Reign Dance

Celebrating God's Kingdom

The Waking

Written and Compiled by
Martin John Nicholls

ISBN 0 85346 167 8
Published by the United Reformed Church
in the United Kingdom
86 Tavistock Place, London WC1H 9RT

Printed by Healeys, 49 - 55 Fore Street, Ipswich IP4 1JL
Cover design by Sara Foyle

For

Matthew and Becca

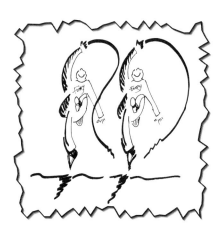

Reign Dance

The Waking

Martin John Nicholls

This collection was drawn together from the rich diversity of worship resources created for and by the young people who visit the Yardley Hastings Centre. They reflect something of the yearning and the yelling; the faith and the fun of being a young person exploring the Christian faith in the United Reformed Church.

The name for this series of books, and of the 25th Anniversary Celebration of FURY held on May 4th 1997, has a considerable significance: FURY has come of age! No longer is the United Reformed Church national youth events programme called *The Walk of Life*. The Fellowship of United Reformed Youth are now celebrating God's Kingdom with a *Reign Dance*!

My thanks go to all those who helped to produce these books, and those who offered contributions. May the challenge and comfort of God's call be heard through these words and ideas.

Martin John Nicholls

Martin

FURY

Published by The Fellowship of United Reformed Youth

Contents

Airs and Graces
Some lively new "Thank you" songs for meal times!

The Colours Of Love

This is one of the weekend liturgies written for use at The Yardley Hastings Centre. The four attitudes of worship - Adoration, Confession, Thanksgiving and Supplication reflect our Reformed liturgy and our need to express our love of God in different ways within the relationship of faith: "I love you!", "I am sorry!", "Thank you!", "Please help!". They also provide a helpful, developing theme and consistant reminder as the worship is offered on Friday evening, Saturday morning, Saturday evening and Sunday Morning.

Each time of worship involves some movement and each person receives a ribbon of the appropriate colour. Purple (The royal colour) for Adoration, Blue (the "Blues") for Confession, Yellow for Thanksgiving (from the tradition of tying yellow ribbons on gate posts as a sign of reconciliation and home-coming), and Red for Intercession (which is a strong symbol of blood, righteous anger, danger and of course the AIDS/ HIV Awareness ribbons).

The ribbons can be worn around the wrist, (or anywhere else!) giving a corporate focus to the worship shared until the next prayer time, when they can be tied to a prayer tree (a bare branch) or similar focal point and the next colour can be shared and worn. In this way, the bare branch becomes progressively colourful and "blossoms" with each offer of prayer.

The group should be sitting in a square, with each side making the North, South, East or West responses. Where possible the room should be in candle light with suitable quiet music creating a peaceful atmosphere. (Ribbons can be obtained very cheaply from local florists and torn into thin strips.)

For the whole weekend you will need:

> Ribbons for everyone in Purple, Blue, Yellow and Red
> A bare branch as a Prayer Tree
> Background music
> A Bible
> Floating candles
> Night Light candles
> Large glass bowl of water
> A cloth or blanket to lay on the ground
> An old post of wood or a log
> A small cross
> Some 2" nails
> A hammer
> Pens and Paper
> you may also need to ask those taking part to bring a torch and
> a symbol of thanksgiving.

PURPLE FOR ADORATION

You will need purple ribbons, the prayer tree, (a bare branch), some inspiring orchestral background music and a Bible.

Strong orchestral music played quietly

Leader:	This is the place, O God, and this is the time!
All:	**Here and now you wait to break into our experience!**
N:	To change our minds, to change our attitudes;
S:	To change our ways, to change our lives!
E:	To help us see the whole of life with your eyes;
W:	To hear your Word for our own time!
Leader:	To help us smell the fragrance of your glory;
N:	To breathe in the freshness of your Holy Spirit!
S:	To help us reach out and touch the face of Jesus;
E:	To feel your healing touch and taste your mercy!
W:	To discover you in the unexpected;
All:	**To worship you with our whole selves!**
Leader:	This is the place -
All:	**as are all places!**
Leader:	This is the time -
All:	**as are all times!**
Leader:	Here and now we come to worship our Creator.
All:	**Come, Spirit of God, we await your power and your presence!**

Alan Gaunt and Martin John Nicholls

Song: Come among us, living Lord

Come among us, living Lord,
we come to hear your living word.
We meet together in the name of Christ
to share your mission and your sacrifice;
to receive the power which only you can give,
that we might live.
Come fill this time of silence!

Martin John Nicholls (can be sung to the tune Sound of Silence by Paul Simon)

We kneel in silence and all are invited to offer one word of adoration to God in a whisper e.g. "Creator", "Sovereign", "Saviour", "Guide"...

Silence

God's Word: Psalm 139. Verses 1-6.

A whispered prayer:

N: You know what they are saying, Lord,
S: Some say that you're not there;
E: Some say that you don't love us;
W: Some say that you don't care.
N: Some say you're dead, or far away,
S: Some say that they're not sure;
E.   Some say they don't know how to pray
W: and want to know much more.
N: Some say they can't believe in you,
S: They don't know who to trust;
E: We come to say we do believe...
W: That *you* believe in *us!*
All: You believe in us! You believe in us...

As we continue to whisper the last line over and over,
we share and wear the Purple Ribbons, the royal colour, for Adoration.

Silence

A Song

We bless each other by embracing our sisters and brothers and saying:

God has made you and believes in you, be faithful.

BLUE FOR CONFESSION

*You will need blue ribbons, the prayer tree, a Bible, some blues background music (instrumental),
enough night lights or small floating candles for one each and a large glass bowl of water.*

Quiet music is played

Leader: How dare you!
You, the sculptor of mountains, have shaped our horizons.
N: You, the painter of rainbows, have coloured our characters.
S: You, the weaver of seasons, have wrapped us in your goodness.
E: You, the juggler of galaxies, have caught us when we have fallen.
W: You, the composer of life have entrusted us with your symphony
of creation!

N: How dare you reach out and touch us when you know we are unclean.
S: How dare you choose us when you know we are so weak.
E: How dare you believe in us when our faith is so fragile.
W: How dare you forgive us when we make the same mistakes again
and again.
Leader: How dare you love us so completely when our love for you is so
conditional.

All: How dare you!

Silence

You are God.
God is love.
Love makes all things new.
We adore you!

Song: Come among us, living Lord

Come among us, living Lord,
we come to hear your living word.
We meet together in the name of Christ
to share your mission and your sacrifice;
to receive the power which only you can give,
that we might live.
Come fill this time of silence!

Martin John Nicholls (can be sung to the tune Sound of Silence by Paul Simon)

Silence

N: Excuses. Excuses.
S: Conditions. Compromise.
E: Apathy. Arrogance.
W: Selfishness. Short Cuts.
N: Eyes
All: **Closed!**
S: Ears
All: **Closed!**
E: Hearts
All: **Closed!**
W: Wallets
All: **Closed!**
           God, forgive us.
           We are so sorry.

Silence

God's Word: Psalm 139. Verses 7-12.

We each come forward and light a candle to symbolise the things we wish to confess to God. We bring the candles to a central place or float them in the water, dipping our fingers in the water as a symbol of God's forgiveness.

A Song

The music or song continues as we tie our purple ribbons to the prayer tree and share and wear the blue ribbons for Confession.

Leader: Lord Jesus, you came to show us the Father;
           You came to give us hope;
           You came with healing in your fingertips,
           love in your heart and forgiveness on your lips.

All: **Loving Lord, dare we be different for you?**

N: We come to show you our failure.
           We come because we lose hope.
           We come with fingers clenched into fists,
           greed in our hearts and hatred on our lips.

All: **Loving Lord, dare we be different for you?**

S: You came sensitively, putting the needs of others first.
           We come blatantly, taking what we want.
           You came revealing what is possible in a human life.
           We come satisfied with second, or third best.

All: **Loving Lord, dare we be different for you?**

E: You came offering life.
We come struggling to exist.
You came showing us God's Kingdom in every word and gesture.
We come showing a faith watered down by complacency and comfort.

All: **Loving Lord, dare we be different for you?**

W: Call us by name to follow you.
Touch us with the love that burns and heals.
Speak to us with the words that wash us clean.
Refresh us.
Make us new.

All: **Loving Lord, dare we be different for you?**
Show us again what love demands.
Show us again what your people need.
Dare us to take risks:
To make a stand;
To make amends;
To make a difference;
To make the Gospel real today.
For your glory,
let it be so!

We bless each other by embracing our sisters and brothers and saying:

God has forgiven you, be faithful.

YELLOW FOR THANKSGIVING

You will need yellow ribbons, a Bible, night light candles for everyone, quiet background music and a blanket or table cloth laid out in the centre of the room. You may also ask everyone to bring with them a torch and/or a small symbol of their thanksgiving to God e.g. photograph, glasses, ring, watch, keys ... items which point beyond themselves to a deeper thankfulness.

Quiet Music is played. The room is in darkness. One by one we light our candles.

Leader:	Once it was dark
All:	**But now light has dawned upon us.**
	Thank God!
N:	Once it was cold
All:	**But now the warmth embraces us.**
	Praise God!
S:	Once it was winter
All:	**But now Spring has come.**
	Worship our creator!
E:	Once the world seemed lifeless
All:	**But now new life is bursting from the ground.**
	God is faithful!
W:	Once we were no people
All:	**But now we are God's people.**
	A royal priesthood, called by God's Spirit!
Leader:	Once we were dead
All:	**But now we are alive!**
	Jesus is Lord!

Song: Come among us, living Lord

Come among us, living Lord,
we come to hear your living word.
We meet together in the name of Christ
to share your mission and your sacrifice;
to receive the power which only you can give,
that we might live.
Come fill this time of silence!

Martin John Nicholls (can be sung to the tune Sound of Silence by Paul Simon)

Silence

We each move to the centre and place our candles and our symbols of thanksgiving on the cloth. We may wish to add a brief word explaining the significance of our symbol.

God's Word: Psalm 139. Verses 13-18.

A Song

As the song or music continues quietly, we begin to give thanks for each other.

If torches are available, they can be shone at the feet of each person, in turn, whilst the group gives thanks for that person in silence or out loud. Alternatively, the group could pass round a single candle and as each person receives it, so the others hold out their hands, one by one (as if offering a gift) and give thanks for one gift or attribute that person has brought to the group.

A Creed for today...

Leader:	We believe in God, In Jesus Christ, In the Holy Spirit, And in you and me.
N:	We believe the Holy Spirit has freed us to worship as a community.
S:	We believe the Holy Spirit works through balloons and ministers,
E:	Daisies and wiggly children, clanging cymbals and silence,
W:	Drama and the unexpected, choirs and banners,
N:	Touching and praying, spontaneity and planning,
S:	Faith and doubt, tears and laughter,
E:	Leading and supporting, hugging and kneeling,
W:	Dancing and stillness, applauding and giving,
N:	Creativity and plodding, words and listening,
S:	Holding and letting go, thank you and help me,
E:	Scriptures and alleluias, agonising and celebrating,
W:	Accepting and caring, through you and through me, through Love.
Leader:	We believe God's Holy Spirit lives in this community of dancing, hand holding people where lines of age, politics and lifestyles are crossed.
N:	We believe in praising God for life.
S:	We believe in responding to God's grace.
E:	We believe in the poetry within each of us.
W:	We believe in dreams and visions.
Leader:	We believe in old people running and children leading.
ALL:	**We believe in the Kingdom of God within us.** **We believe in Love.**

Source unknown

We tie our blue ribbons to the prayer tree and share and wear the yellow ribbons for Thanksgiving.

We bless each other by embracing our sisters and brothers and saying:

Thank God for you, be faithful.

RED FOR SUPPLICATION

You will need red ribbons, a Bible, Nails, a hammer, pieces of torn paper, an old wooden post
or log (or door), pens, quiet music (such as a song of protest or social concern) a lighted candle or
small cross to pass round and three readers prepared to share the sketch "Three's Company" No.16

Quiet music is played

A Passing Prayer:
We each read a line of the prayer and everyone makes the responses in bold.
A candle or a small cross can be passed round too, to symbolise the sharing of concern
and to indicate who reads next.

Good morning, Lord! We come to you
    Called by the creating one.
We are unready and unworthy
    Forgiven by the loving one.
We face another day
    Refreshed by the healing one.
Assured of your presence, peace and power
    Found by the searching one.
Seeking your will and unfolding your kingdom
    Inspired by the guiding one.
Standing in your strength and not our own
    Humbled by the serving one.

Song: *Come among us, living Lord*

Come among us, living Lord,
we come to hear your living word.
We meet together in the name of Christ
to share your mission and your sacrifice;
to receive the power which only you can give,
that we might live.
Come fill this time of silence!

Martin John Nicholls (can be sung to the tune Sound of Silence by Paul Simon)

Silence

The Passing Prayer continues:

Let us be your people today
    In our words and in our actions.
Let us practise what we preach
    Today and every day.
Let us follow in the footsteps of Christ
    Here, there and everywhere.

Let us dare to be different and dare to dream
With these people and all people.
Let us put away our self pity and self indulgence
Humbled by the serving one.
Let us be discerning and decisive
Courageous and Christ-like.
Let us be your church
Reformed and reforming.

Silence

We pray for those who share this morning, this place, this life with us.
Our families, our friends, our colleagues.
Those far away and those sitting beside us.
Those we love and those we find it difficult to love.
Those who will face a difficult decision today
Those who will face a new challenge today.
Those whose day will be full of love and liberation
Those whose day will be just the same as any other day.
Those who will lead our nation today
Those who will mould public opinion today.
Those who will write what others read today
Those who will stand and fight for justice and truth today.
Those whose jobs will give them too much to do today
Those whose unemployment will give them nothing to do today.

Silence

God of all time, and this time;
all people, and these people;
all places and this place,
we offer this day,
it's promise,
it's purpose,
and its potential,
to you.

By the power of your Holy Spirit,
transform it from the mundane into the miraculous;
from the ordinary into the extraordinary!

Amen! Amen! AMEN!

A Song

God's Word: "Three's Company" (No.16)

Silence

In the footsteps of Martin Luther, we each take a piece of torn paper and write on it one thing that we would like to see changed in our lives, our church, our world. We then take turns in nailing our "reforms" to the post or "door" as the music plays.

We tie our yellow ribbons to the prayer tree and share and wear the red ribbons of Supplication. These are not added to the tree but worn by everyone as they leave the place of worship and go out into the world to be used in the answers to their prayers.

Leader: Nothing is more important!
All: **Nothing is more urgent!**
N: Nothing is more powerful!
All: **Nothing is more profound!**
S: Nothing is more comforting!
All: **Nothing is more challenging!**
E: Nothing is more fulfilling!
All: **Nothing is more exciting -**
W: Than what we do today:

> **We worship the living God;**
> **We accept God's call on our lives;**
> **We offer ourselves to serve God's people**
> **in God's world,**
> **in God's strength,**
> **in God's love**
> **in the name of Jesus!**
> **Amen!**

We bless each other by embracing our sisters and brothers and saying:

God has called you, be faithful.

Yearnings and Burnings
Prayers and Meditations from the heart

So where is the joy?

Each verse of this prayer could be read by a different voice with the group responding with
the words in bold. The group begins by sitting in a circle, then kneeling and standing.
A song and dance could follow...!

Living God, we praise you!
For this astounding planet
in this awesome universe;
for your inspiring creation
and incredible son;
for our freedom
and our future!
We are not worthy!

(sitting)

So where is the joy?
Why aren't we dancing?
When does the singing begin?

Loving God, we adore you!
For your attention to detail;
your brilliant timing;
your knowledge of us
and love for us.
We are not worthy!

(kneeling)

So where is the joy?
Why aren't we dancing?
When does the singing begin?

Liberating God, we worship you!
Humbled by your glory;
moved by your majesty;
intrigued by your Kingdom
and touched by your truth.
We are not worthy!

(standing)

So where is the joy?
Why aren't we dancing?
When does the singing begin?

Living, loving, liberating God,
forgive our humanness,
our doubts, our reluctance,
half-heartedness and apathy.

Help us to see beyond
our childish, fairy-tale
charicatures of you.
Here and now, may we worship you
in silence and shouting,
music and dancing.
For you are real!
You are worthy!
You are!

Amen!

Nicky Turnbull and Martin John Nicholls

The Desert of Prayer

A central table or cloth with dry sand, forming a small dune, makes an intriguing focal point.
During the meditation, small flowers could be placed into the sand, causing the desert to "bloom".
Alternatively glass beads or other "treasures" could be buried in the sand and "unearthed"
during worship. A time of open prayer follows this meditation naturally ...

My child,
Why do you say: "I cannot pray!"
Do you think you are alone?

You are not the first to enter the desert.
Look down at the sand at your feet,
and see the many footprints all around you.
Footprints made by the souls of history.
They also felt alone.
They also found prayer difficult.

Consider:
In this desert
Abraham roamed.
He was homeless.
He had left his security to follow my call.
He travelled, uncertain of the future, afraid.

In this desert
Joseph was abandoned.
He was betrayed by his family.
He dreamed alone.

In this desert
Moses lived.
Haunted by his past.
Humbled by his present.
Daunted by what was expected of him.

In this desert
David hid.
He was hunted.
Misunderstood and misrepresented.
He learned how to be patient.

In this desert
Elijah sat.
He was tired.
He had carried God's message for so long.
He felt he had nothing left to give.

In this desert
The Son of God wandered.
He was tempted.
He came face to face with God.
He came face to face with himself.
He was offered so many alternatives.
He chose the cross.

In this desert
many great people have walked.
Feeling lost.
Feeling they have failed.
Alone.
Disappointed.
Confused.
Exhausted.

Now, my child,
lift your head from the dust,
see, your wilderness is far from deserted!
You stand in the midst of a huge crowd of travellers
of every culture,
and every walk of life!

Open your eyes, my child,
and look around you.
You may see your friends and your family,
those whom you know and love,
for all journey into the desert at some time.

Lift your eyes, my child,
and look into mine.
I am with you too.
I am always with you.
You are never alone.

Now...pray to me...

Tim Lowe

I feel so lonely, Lord

A lighted candle in a circle of nails, or barbed wire, makes a challenging focal point.

I feel so lonely, Lord
like I'm shut away from everything.
I feel excluded.
Unwanted.
It's like that feeling of being in a crowd -
and yet being so alone.

"It'll pass"
"It just takes time"

I know all that,
I've heard it all before -
too many times.
But it's now; here and now,
and it hurts.

No-one understands,
no-one is feeling the pain I'm feeling.
No-one can.

And then I remember you...

I remember your last days:
I hear the shouts of the soldiers.
I catch the look in your eyes as they spit and jeer.
I see those who loved you turn away one by one.
I watch you.
You never give in.
I feel the searing pain of the whip,
the gnawing agony of the cross,
the terror...humility...shame...

and then I cry.

Only then do I remember
that you have been here;
you've done it all.
You've suffered all this
and more horribly than I could ever imagine.
You have lived my life, Lord,
and experienced my suffering.

Thank you, Lord, that someone does understand.

Be with me.

Nicky Turnbull

The answer's 'Yes'...

Those praying may like to hold their hands open, as if offering or receiving a gift...

I'm sure I can hear you, Lord,
Feel you too.

It isn't warm - not as I'd expected it to be
but it isn't harsh either,
it's just real...

It's the only thing that feels constant,
a realisation that neither changes nor develops,
just sits - in my heart.

Sometimes I'm aware of it and contemplate it,
other times I just let it exist without thought.

But I don't forget it, Lord,
I don't dismiss it.
It's the most sincere, unfeigned knowledge
I have ever known.

I don't know when it came,
perhaps it was always there.
It's just that my eyes are wiser now - more focused.

It will surface when the time's right,
it will have to - for all our sakes;
Mine.
Yours.

Thank you, Lord, for the awakening,
for the invitation.
I'm not worthy...
but you know that.

And, Lord,

the answer's 'Yes' ...
but you know that too.

I think that's why you asked.

Nicky Turnbull

Just like Jesus

A plastic hoop makes an excellent frame for a large "Dream Catcher".
Each person writes their dreams for the world, church, themselves on ribbons before tying them to the
frame and weaving them through each others ribbons. This could then be hung up as a focal point.

Holy God!
When you sent your son
he amazed, challenged
inspired and even shocked.
He unveiled a radical lifestyle.
He revealed the potential for peace.
He began to unfold your Kingdom for us.

As we look at our world,
at the injustice, oppression and violence
all around us,
our purpose becomes clearer and clearer.

Help us not to be satisfied
with the way things are.
Dare us not to accept second best.
Forgive our selfish complacency
and stifling comfort.

Guide us, not to be *more* like Jesus,
but *just* like Jesus:
Amazing, challenging;
Inspiring, shocking;
Defiantly different!
Powerfully peaceful!

Give us the audacity to love
without condition!
Give us the courage
to stand up and be counted!
Give us the voices
to speak up for the powerless.
Give us the arms
to lift the weak.

We have caught your dream of a better world;
take and use us to build it!

Amen.

Nicky Turnbull and Martin John Nicholls

North American Indians wove "Dream Catchers" to protect their lodges from bad dreams.
Christians sometimes need help in catching the good dreams and visions and turning them into reality!

In Love

*This meditation is very moving when shared under a clear night sky, with everyone lying on
their backs looking up at the stars. An alternative is to read it in candlelight with music
from Holst's Planet Suite played in the background.*

In the beginning
your Word was in creation.

Moving with it,
exploding and merging
with neutrons and protons;
swirling and spinning
with planets and stars.

Growing with it,
multiplying and replicating
with molecules and microbes;
reproducing and evolving
with cells and organisms.

Into the world
your Son was born.
Living, breathing.
Flesh and bone.
Crying and laughing
with parents and family.

Serving, teaching, loving,
with friends and enemies.

Hanging and suffering
with blood and nails.

In love
your Son died for the world.
In love
Jesus was raised from death.
In love
you offer forgiveness and healing;
new life and new beginnings
to your world . . .
to us.

In Jesus
we see your character
in ways that we can begin to grasp.

Perfect love,
embracing and nurturing
every creature.
Every life.
Appreciating us.
Smiling at us.
Crying with us.

In our lives
you continue the miracle
of creation.
Moving and growing.
Living and serving.

With the dazzle of each new sunrise
the world is given light.
With the beauty of each new moonrise
the world is given rest.
With the treasure of each new birth
the world is given hope.
With the gift of each new moment
the world is given an opportunity
to know you as God,
respect your fragile creation
and to be your faithful stewards.

Let it be so.

Tim Lowe

Hello. Lord!

A prayer for two children or young people who are known to have very different personalities!

1.   Hello, Lord!
     It's me, the noisy one!
     I have come to worship you,
     and to thank you
     for giving me a voice
     and the confidence to use it!

2.   Hello, Lord!
     It's me, the quiet one!
     I have come to worship you too,
     and to thank you
     for giving me ears
     and the confidence to use them!

1.   You are such a wonderful God:
     You spoke and the world happened;
     You raised your voice and the universe took shape;
     You shouted and the stars began to dance;
     You laughed because it was all so good;
     You called me, and I came to you.

2.   You are such a loving God:
     You listen to my prayers;
     You know my secret thoughts;
     You see everything I do;
     You whisper your ways to me in dreams
     and imagination;
     You wait patiently for me to understand
     and to respond.

1.   The roll of the thunder and the crash of the sea...
2.   The caress of a breeze and the fall of a rain drop...
1.   The glory of the sunrise and roar of the waterfall...
2.   The wings of a butterfly and the ripple of a stream...
1.   All these are yours.
2.   All these are beautiful.
1.   All these speak of your love.
2.   We join our hearts with your whole creation;
1.   With a shout or a whisper;
2.   In doing and waiting;

Both: We worship you, our God!
1.   *(Shouting)* AMEN!
2.   *(Whispering)* Amen.

Martin John Nicholls, Clare Reeder and Greta Knowles

Reign Dance   **The Waking**

Acts of Faith
Sketches, dialogues and other useful stuff...

The chain of life...

This comical little story works best if the verses are read alternately be two readers
who are well rehearsed and willing to play up to the accents. It can be enhanced by having
5 children or young people dressed as the characters and saying the dialogue themselves!

There was a man whose name was Fred
who drove a big red bus.
"A friendly bloke", or so they said,
"who never made a fuss!"

"Costs nothing to be cheerful"
Fred would say, with a chuckle and a smile.
He'd tell you jokes, and sometimes sing
for mile after mile after mile!

Then one day people noticed
something different about Fred:
"P'raps he's got a headache,
or was he late to bed?"

"Perhaps our Fred is feeling sick,
but Fred is never ill!"
Whatever caused it, Fred was rude,
especially to Bill.

Now Bill was an accountant
for a company in town
and he had a secretary
whose name was Rita Brown

Because of Fred, Bill got cross
and yelled and poor old Rita
who spilled her coffee, dropped her files
and thought her boss might beat her!

By lunch time she was furious,
her mind was in a jumble.
"I'm off to lunch!" she said to Bill
in quite a forceful mumble.

At the café she began
to argue with the waiter:
"The fish is off, the soup is cold,
and so is the potata !"

The waiter was Luigi
who put up with a lot:
customers who ordered
what the kitchen hadn't got;

moaning that the service
or the food was really bad.
So hearing Rita grumble
made poor Luigi mad:

He stormed into the kitchen
like a wild, raging stallion.
Throwing pots and pans around
and swearing...in Italian!

"Mama mia!" he complained
"I can't serve any faster!"
Then, as if to prove the point,
he dropped a plate of pasta!

This was just the final straw,
and though it may sound silly,
he lay there in the bolognese
blaming it on Lily!

Now Lily was the little cook
who only worked part-time.
Her name was really Gladys,
but Gladys doesn't rhyme!

It wasn't Lily's fault, of course,
but she got all the blame.
Across the kitchen she could hear
him slandering her name.

She had really had enough;
she packed her things to go:
"I've had enough of this!" she said.
(There, I told you so).

She turned from laughing Lily
into someone sour and surly.
"I'm giving up this job" she said,
and stormed off home...early.

That evening Lily's husband
came home for his tea.
He walked in through the front door
and called out cheerily:

"Hello, love! What a night!
Got caught up in this fog!"
"That's your problem" Lily snapped,
"Your dinner's in the dog!"

"I've had a rotten day" she cried,
"And now I'm off to bed!"
He seemed surprised, I don't know why,
'cause her husband's name was FRED!

Jesus said, "Love others,
as I always love you"
Easy enough to say it,
but how hard it is to do!

'Cause life's a chain reaction:
we give out what we get;
we've passed it on since Adam
and we cannot break it yet!

Loving someone means that we
should try to share their pain,
not take it out on someone else,
but bravely break the chain.

Are you like Fred, sometimes pushing
back at those who shove you?
Or can you say, like Jesus,
"I forgive you, and I love you"?

Amazing Grace!

A bringing together of two powerful parables of Jesus which reveal intriguing facets of the Kingdom of God - the Parable of the Great Banquet (Luke 14. 15-24) and the Parable of the Workers in the Vineyard (Matthew 20. 1-16). Well rehearsed, this dialogue could be played with the two actors meeting in the street and relentlessly telling their respective stories to each other - shouting the lines they have in common simultaneously. Otherwise they could stand apart, each telling their tale to the audience, oblivious to the other actor. (To <u>really</u> make it live, the lines should be learned!)

1. It was amazing!
2. It was amazing!

1. There I was with nowhere to go...
2. There I was with nothing to do...

1. When all of a sudden I receive this invitation...
2. When all of a sudden I receive this invitation...

1. "Come to the Master's Banquet!"
2. "Come and work in the Master's Vineyard!"

1. I thought, "Wow!"
2. I thought, "Wow!"

1. Why me?
2. Why me?

1. I mean, I'm not exactly rich and powerful...
2. I mean, I'm not exactly skilled and qualified...

1. I nearly didn't go...
2. I nearly didn't go...

1. But to be honest, I needed a meal.
2. To be honest, I needed a job.

1. I was hungry, you see...
2. I was hungry, you see...

1. So, anyway, I accepted.
2. So, anyway, I accepted.

1. Beautiful place it was, and so much food.
2. Beautiful place it was, and so much space.

1. There were all sorts of people there...
2. There were all sorts of people there...

1. People I'd never seen before!
2. People I'd never want to see again!

1. I kept picking the wrong cutlery!
2. I kept picking the wrong grapes!

1. But the Master didn't mind...
2. But the Master didn't mind...

1. We ate for three solid hours...
2. We worked for three solid hours...

1. It felt so good...!
2. It felt so good...!

1. Then I found out that some others had been invited earlier.
2. Then I found out that some others had been invited earlier.

1. And they'd all said they'd come... at the agreed time.
2. And they'd all said they'd come... at the agreed wage.

1. Only later, they all made their excuses...
2. Only later, they all made their protests...

1. They said they had more important things to do...
2. They said they were more important than us...

1. They didn't like it because the Master treated us the same...
2. They didn't like it because the Master rewarded us the same...

1. Strange that...
2. Strange that...

1. 'Cause like the Master said, "I want my house to be full".
2. 'Cause like the Master said, "I want those who came last to have the same as those who came first".

1. We didn't deserve it...
2. We didn't deserve it...

1. But the Master is just so generous...!
2. But the Master is just so generous...!

1. Amazing!

(pause)

2. Grace!

Christmas Rapping

A great new way to re-tell the age old story of Christ's birth which even includes something
of the role of the Old Testament characters!
This rap was first performed as part of a Family Festival Service with the children and young
people dressed in baseball caps, sun glasses etc and looking so cool! The piece really needs a drum
machine (found in many modern keyboards) or a solid live drum rhythm to make it work.
Verses, lines, even odd words can be allocated to different groups and individuals to emphasise
certain points of the story and add interest to the overall sound. But it does need practice!

Now this is the story all about how
God came to the world and turned it upside down.
Just let me tell you all about the story of
God's plan! God's power! God's Son! God's love!

Since time began, every woman and man
has tried to live in harmony as best they can
but we're still too proud; we're still too greedy;
we help ourselves and not the poor and the needy

And that's why God kinda intervened
and said, "Hey! Listen up! Let me tell you what it means
to be the people of the one true God up above
you gotta give and forgive, gotta live, gotta love!"

But the people said, "How?" 'cause they didn't have a clue
so God said, "O.K. then, I'll tell you what I'll do -
I'll make with you a covenant, and I'll hold you in my hand,
and I'll show you some signs that even you will understand!"

So the Lord sent leaders and the Lord sent kings
and the Lord sent prophets who did lots of strange things:
There was Amos and Micah and Joel and Isaiah,
Ezekiel and Habbakkuk and Jerry Jeremiah.

But the people didn't listen. They didn't have ears.
So they made the same mistakes for years and years.
'Till God said, "Wo! I know what must be done -
there's nothin' left to do except to introduce my son!"

So he said, "Yo, Joseph!" and he said, "Yo, Mary!
Some things are gonna happen and they're gonna be scary,
just do as I say!" And he sent them
for a weekend away in Bethlehem!

So they packed their mule and they headed on down
to D.A.V.I.D.'S. town
'cause Joseph was descended from Israel's king
and Caesar said he wanted a census thing.

But the town was full; the inns were full;
the rooms and the tables and the bins were full.
So Mary and Joe were getting ready to go
when the keeper of the inn shouted out, "Hey, no!"

He took 'em out back to a tumble-down shack
that was really in need of some Shake and Vac
and there, in the stable, they huddled and they shivered;
Joseph had to stand while Mary delivered!

Into our poverty; into our life;
into our struggle and into our strife;
into the world a new age dawned
as Jesus, the Son of God was born!

Martin John Nicholls and the Children of Yardley Hastings Junior Church

Star Trek

The sequel to number 14, Christmas Rapping, all the same notes and suggestions apply!

In the East, at the time, there were three or four guys.
They were healthy and wealthy and hey, were they wise!
They spent their nights with their eyes on the skies
and they watched and they waited 'till "What a surprise!"

It was big! It was bright! It was whiter than white!
An awesome star, and it lit up the night!
As the dudes were deciding what they should do,
well, lo and behold, the star started to move!

It was here a star, there a star, everywhere a star. Ha!
They jumped on their camels ('cause they didn't have a car) Ha!
They followed it high. They followed it low.
They followed that star 'cause they didn't know
where they should go. No, no, no.
So they followed it fast and they followed it slow
and they ran out of rhymes so they shouted "Yo!"

They travelled by night and they travelled by day
right over the hills and far, far away
till the star pulled up, and they did too,
at the inn and the stable and you-know-who!

This was the moment they had waited for
so they parked their camels and they walked through the door
with frankincense and myrrh and gold,
strange gifts for a baby just a few days old...

...but gold, I'm told, is the coolest thing
you can give to the son of the mighty king,
and frankincense is a sign of prayer,
and myrrh is a symbol of death. Well, yeah...

O.K. this was God who came down to earth
to share our death as well as our birth;
to share our laughter and to share our pain
so we never have to feel afraid or lonely again!

'Cause God is here, we're in God's hands.
He walked this earth and he understands.
God loves with love that will never cease -
just look at his son, the Fresh Prince of Peace!

Those guys were cool, and they really knew
what they should bring; what they should do.
'Cause only the best is good enough
to give to the one who shows God's love.

They were wise for looking for something new;
they were wise for discovering the signs were true;
they were wise for bringing their gifts along too!
They looked for Jesus! The wise still do!

Martin John Nicholls and the Children of Yardley Hastings Junior Church

Three's Company

*This simple script brings together three very different friends of Jesus who have something
in common - meeting him! The piece can be based around a step ladder with Zacchaeus sitting
at the top, Mary Magdalene standing stage right and Peter leaning on the steps. They each talk
straight to the audience, unaware of each other. They smile and take their time as they reminisce...*

Z. This is a very special place for me.
P. This is a very special place for me.
M. This used to be a good place for me.

Z. Oh, Sorry! My name's Zacchaeus!
P. By the way, my name's Peter.
M. My name is Mary.

Z. I used to be a tax collector.
P. I used to be a fisherman.
M. I used to be...umm, self employed.

Z. They used to call me all the names under the sun!
P. They used to call me Simon.
M. They used to call me anything they wanted to.

Z. Now they call me stupid!
P. Now they call me *The Rock.*
M. Now they call me a woman.

Z. I was really caught up in my work.
P. I was really caught up in myself.
M. I was really caught.

Z. I wanted to be something
P. I wanted to be somebody.
M. I wanted to be *me*!

Z. I dreamed of being popular.
P. I dreamed of being different.
M. I dreamed of being free.

Z. But is all seemed so hopeless.
P. But it all seemed so hopeless.
M. It was hopeless.

Z. I only knew how to cheat.
P. I only knew how fish.
M. I only knew how to sell myself.

Z.   It can be lonely at the top.
P.   It can be lonely at sea.
M.   I was lonely.

Z.   Then I met Jesus!
P.   Then I met Jesus!
M.   Then I met Jesus!

Z.   He looked up and saw me, *here*!
P.   He looked over and saw me, *here*!
M.   He *noticed* me!

Z.   He called me by my name... and changed my life!
P.   He called me by my name... and changed my name!
M.   He called me by my name... he called me *Mary*!

Z.   He called me his friend!
P.   He called me his right-hand-man!
M.   He called me *Mary*!

Z.   He offered me a better way.
P.   He offered me a better future.
M.   He offered me... real love.

Z.   He gave me another chance.
P.   He gave me a purpose.
M.   He gave me... hope.

Z.   He showed me what's important.
P.   He showed me what's possible.
M.   He showed me... God.

It's not fair!

A lively version of the parable of the workers in the vineyard Matthew 20. 1-16. Narrator 1 is a clear reader who just wants to get on with the job of telling the story; Narrator 2 is a childlike innocent who can't wait to join in at any opportunity! The Owner should be dressed as a farmer and the group of workers in black clothes with battered straw hats.

1. *(As if reading from the Bible)* Once there was a man...
2. *(Shouting and interrupting)* The Kingdom of Heaven is like this!
1. Not yet!
2. *(Embarrassed)* Sorry!
1. *(Resuming)* Once there was a man who got up very early in the morning...
2. *(Shouting even louder)* The Kingdom of Heaven is like this!
1. What?
2. *(Shouting again)* The Kingdom of Heaven is like this!
1. The Kingdom of Heaven is like <u>what</u>?
2. *(Thinking hard)* The...umm...Kingdom of Heaven is like a man...who got up very early in the morning...?
1. *(Sighing heavily, patience wearing thin)* Once there was a man who got up very early in the morning to hire some labourers to worker in his vineyard...
2. The Kingdom of...
1. *(Interrupting, and through gritted teeth)* Don't even <u>think</u> about it!
2. *(Mouthing silently and grimacing to audience)* Sorry!
1. He agreed to pay them all the regular wage, a silver coin a day...
2. Not much for a day's work is it...?
1. Enough to feed a family for a day.
2. Fair enough.
1. So, he sent them to work in his vineyard...

(Music fades in - e.g. "Israelites" or "Working in a coal mine". Workers dance/mime a tiring, hot, mechanical working movement in formation as they make their way onto stage. They continue their movements as the music fades to a volume which allows the owner to be heard.)

Owner: Excellent, you're working well, but we're not going to get the harvest in before the rains at this rate! We need more hands!

(Workers turn their backs on the audience and freeze. Music continues quietly)

1. So the owner went out again at twelve o'clock and again at three o'clock to hire more workers.
2. It was nearly five o'clock when he went to the market place and saw some people still standing there.
1. How do <u>you</u> know?
2. *(Looking over 1's shoulder at the script)* It says so, there, look!
    (Looks away smugly, even puts thumbs up to the audience)

(Workers each put on their straw hats and take up bored, waiting poses, facing the audience)

Owner: Why are you wasting your time standing round here all day?

Workers: *(A muddle of different shouts all at once)* Nothing else to do...I'm bored
           of sitting at home...waiting for some work...gis a job...I need some money
           ...no one hired us...!

Owner: *(Unable to understand a word)* What?

Workers: *(All shouting together)* NO ONE HIRED US!

Owner: Well, why didn't you say so? Come and work in my vineyard.
           I know it's late but every little helps!

*(Workers remove their hats and continue their working movements. Music fades up
briefly. Workers turn their backs on audience again and freeze)*

1.   When the day was over, the owner called his foreman over...
2.   Was that his name then?
1.   *(Sighing at being interrupted yet again)* What?
2.   "Over"! You said the foreman was called "Over"! Was that his name?

Owner: Start paying the workers what I owe them, starting with those I hired
           last and then pay those I hired first!

(One of the workers becomes the Foreman and begins to pay the workers)

1.   The ones who were hired last each received a silver coin, as agreed,
     but when...
2.   *(Interrupting again)* Just a minute! They'd only worked a few hours in the
     cool of the evening...
1.   That's right, so when the workers who had been working all day stepped
     forward...
2.   They couldn't wait to get their hands on all that dosh!
1.   *(Sighing)* They expected to get more, but...
2.   *(Jumping in, melodramatically)* Oh no! Don't tell me! They all got the <u>same</u>?
1.   They all got the same!
2.   But that's not fair!
1.   That's what <u>they</u> said!

Workers: *(Turning to face the audience and shouting angrily)* That's not fair!
           What do we want? More pay! When do we want it? Now!

(They continue with the shout until the owner speaks)

Owner: All right, all right! I can hear you. I haven't cheated you!

Workers: *(Sarcastically)* Not much!

2.   *(With them all the way)* Not much!

Owner: You agreed to do a day's work for one silver coin, right?

Workers: *(Reluctantly agreeing)* S'pose so.

Owner: Well, I wanted to give those who were called last as much as I have
           given you! Don't I have the right to do as I wish with my own wealth?
           Or are you jealous because I am so generous?

(They freeze)

2. Wow!
1. Jesus told this story, and ended by saying:

All: *(Shouting, clearly)* So those who are last will be first and those who are first will be last!

2. WOW!
1. *(Coughing to attract 2's attention)*
2. *(Returning from his day dream)* Oh, yeah. Right.
   (Clears throat) The Kingdom of heaven is like this!

(1 and 2 shake hands with satisfaction of a job well done)

(All freeze)

Two Little Boys

1. My name is Paul.
2. My name is Paco.

1. I live in Basingstoke.
2. I live in Bogata.

1. I have one brother and one sister.
2. I had three brothers and two sisters, now I have just one brother.

1. My mum and dad look after us.
2. I look after my brother.

1. I live in a house with three bedrooms.
2. I live in a room with three families.

1. I love football! I make my dad take me to watch Arsenal when they're at home.
2. I made a football once, out of a tin and some rags and string.

1. There's a school at the end of my road.
2. There isn't a school for miles.

1. I go every day.
2. I've never been.

1. Sometimes I bunk off!
2. Sometimes I wish I could read.

1. Mum and Dad say that I should go to university.
2. Mum and Dad can't read either.

1. They tell me that education is important. Why?
2. They tell me that education is impossible. Why?

1. I should be free to choose!
2. I should be free to choose!

Nick and Lou Raggett

Bad Taste

First performed at the United Reformed Church's General Assembly, this sketch makes a powerful case for fairly traded goods. Especially coffee. A and B are sitting at identical tables either side of the stage, facing slightly away from each other. Each has a coffee pot, cup and saucer and a jar of instant coffee. B (female) has a jar of Cafédirect. A (male) has a jar of non-fairly traded coffee. They simultaneously pour a cup of coffee, stir in the milk, sit back and sip. Replacing the cup on the saucer they each gaze out across the audience, as if out to sea from a restaurant balcony! C and D are never seen, but there voices need to be heard clearly. Quiet Ardean Pipe music adds to the atmosphere of C and D's words.

A: Breathtaking!

B: Sorry...?

A: Breathtaking!

B: *(Thinking he's referring to her)* Oh! Um, thank you...

A: *(Not noticing her reaction)* The scenery...

B: *(A little deflated)* Oh, yes, the scenery, breathtaking...

They both take another sip and sit back

A: *(taking a deep, satisfied breath)* De-licious!

B: *(Frowning, slightly puzzled)* Sorry...?

A: De-licious!

B: The scenery...?

A: *(In a world of his own)* The meal...

B: *(Not really interested)* Oh, yes, the meal, delicious...

They both take a sip and sit back

A: Beautiful!

B: *(A little impatient now)* Sorry...?

A: Beautiful!

B: *(Raising her voice)* The meal?!

A: *(Same monotone)* Your dress...

B: *(About to lose her temper)* My dress?!! *(Realises the compliment and immediately regains her composure)* Oh! Oh, yes, my dress? Thank you...

They sip and sit back

A: Strange taste though...

B: *(Hackles rising)* I beg your pardon?

A: Strange taste...

B: *(Turns to face him for the first time, about to explode with indignation)* What!?

A: The coffee...

B: *(At the top of her voice)* What about the coffee!!?

A: *(Pausing for effect, then replying quietly and calmly)* Strange taste to the coffee.

She sips her coffee, he smells his.

A: *(As if still tasting the coffee on his tongue)* Bitter...?
B: *(Back in moderate mood, looking away)* No, no...it was just a misunderstandi...
A: *(Interrupting her for the first time)* The coffee...tastes sort of bitter...
B: *(Tasting her own coffee once more)* Mine's perfectly all right. In fact
     (she refills her cup) It's rather good!
A: *(Gazing off into the distance, wondering to himself)* I wonder what it can be...?

They both freeze in position. Andean pipe music fades in quietly.

Voices are heard from behind the audience or over the PA

C: Perhaps you can taste the tears of my children - the two I have left, Marco
     and Rosina. They cry because they do not have enough to eat. Every
     day...every single day, their young bodies cry out for the food they need to
     grow. Their sisters are no more. They died last year, all three. Beautiful girls,
     my beautiful girls. Eva and Maria died of dysentery from the bad water.
     Nina died from measles...just from *measles!* We had no money for medicines.
     Your coffee is bitter? You can taste the tears of my children.

D: I heard my mother singing today. It was good. She was pouring the coffee
     beans onto the drying mats and spreading them out with her hands to dry
     under the sun...and she was singing! Not a song of protest or anger...not a
     song of fear or hatred... not even a song of freedom, but a *free* song she was
     singing! My wife and children heard her dry, tuneless voice, chirping like a
     cracked reed, and they laughed...they *laughed!* Soon the whole co-operative
     was singing with her as we picked the coffee and carried it up the mountain
     to the store sheds. Your coffee tastes good? You can taste our freedom.

Music fades out...

A: *(Coming to life slowly and still tasting something)* Well, it's not good enough!
B: What is isn't?
A: This coffee business, it's simply not good enough!
B: I quite agree...so what do you intend to do about it?
A: I'm going to make a complaint...
B: Really? Good show! To whom...?
A: Waiter!

They freeze. Music returns...

C: Perhaps you can taste the sweat of my body as I work 14 hours a day to meet
     the demands of the company. Perhaps you can taste my wife's blood as she
     picks beans until her swollen fingers bleed. Perhaps you can taste the
     injustice of the large coffee conglomerates holding down the world price of
     coffee to keep up trade, and paying us less and less to do more and more
     work, just to survive. Perhaps you can taste the outrage we feel each time a
     limousine brings another executive to our village to tell us that, due to market
     forces, the company cannot pay us as much as last season. Perhaps you can
     taste our powerlessness as we realise that our children will never go to school,
     we will never have any dignity and our family will never live before we die.

D: Everyday I thank God for Traidcraft. They ensure that we get a fair price for our coffee beans, much higher than before. That means that our co-operative can afford to pay a doctor to look after our members. For myself, the price difference has meant that I can afford more food for my family and send my children to school properly equipped with books for the first time. Traidcraft has given us more than a fair price, it has given us back our self respect, our hope...Your coffee tastes good? You can taste our dignity!

Music fades out...

A: *(Coming back to life and looking over to B hesitantly)* May I...?
B: Sorry...?
A: *(Signalling for a cup of her coffee)* May I...?
B: Yes, of course...*(She pours some coffee into his cup)*
A: *(Tasting it but not wishing to show too much enthusiasm)* Mmmm, not bad... *(He takes the pot from her and fills his cup)*
B: *(Taken aback at his audacity)* Please! help yourself!
A: It's good! Not bitter at all! Bet it costs more though...
B: More than what?
A: More than my brand...
B: A few pence, perhaps, but that's a small price to pay for fair trade don't you think?
A: Er, yes, I suppose so. Still, no point spending more than you have to, eh?

They go back to their original positions

B: *(Sighing at his lack of understanding)* Dense!
A: *(Oblivious)* Sorry...?
B: The undergrowth...
A: *(Slightly puzzled)* Oh!

They freeze

Are you MAD?!

Written for a presentation at The East Midlands Provincial Synod, this sketch embraces
many attitudes stifling local churches today. Four couples appear from different points around
the building. They begin their conversations as they enter, before striking a pose and freezing
on stage as A, C, E and G say the word "mad!" in each short scene. Standing in a central position,
B, D, F and H should reflect their vulnerability whilst their partners show their annoyance, anger,
irritation...! Once all four couples are on stage, the sketch continues with each couple, in turn, coming to
life and continuing their story. The dialogues should move along at a natural pace without rushing.
* A large focal point of the letters M.A.D. would help!

(A and B enter)

A. You're going *where*?
B. To see Louise...
A. Louise? But I didn't think you two were talking to each other...
B. Well, yes, we broke up months ago actually...
A. Word is that she was awful to you. No-one would blame you if you never
   spoke to her again!
B. Mmm, it's not going to be easy, but I think I ought to try to...you know...make
   the first move...hold out the olive branch...
A. But you *know* what she's like...you're wasting your time!
B. Maybe, but I'm going to give it a try.
A. Well, I think you're *mad*!

(They freeze)

(C and D enter)

C. I hear they actually passed the plans at last night's meeting!
D. Yep! Finally! It's exciting isn't it? Now the real work begins!
C. You can say that again! *How* much is it going to cost?
D. About £100,000 altogether. Quite a challenge eh? It'll certainly test our faith!
C. And your bank accounts! Do you really think that a church like yours can
   raise that sort of money? After all, the new hall's going to be used by other
   people too!
D. Well, they do believe in the project...I think they'll come up trumps!
C. Do you know what I think? I think they're *mad*!

(They freeze)

(E and F enter)

E. You're still with us, then! I thought you'd already gone!
F. Flying out next Tuesday.
E. And where is it you're going?
F. Near Rangoon.
E. Oh, Africa!
F. Myanmar, actually.
E. Oh, *that* Rangoon! Yes, of course, Myanmar...it's still abroad, though isn't it?

F. Yes, and that's why I'm looking forward to it!

E. What will you be doing exactly?

F. Oh, basic medical care mostly, you know, travelling round villages, giving injections, helping the regular medical teams...

E. It all sounds a bit risky. Hasn't there been some trouble out there recently, and what about all those tropical diseases and creepy crawlies? Wouldn't you rather just join the Community Team at Yardley Hastings?

F. Yes, they said it could be dangerous, but then, so could Yardley Hastings - two of my friends were there and said it changed their lives...!

E. Well, rather you than me. Personally, I think you must be _mad_!

(They freeze)

(G and H enter)

G. I didn't like that one bit!

H. Didn't you?

G. No, I didn't...did you?

H. Well, I found it quite stimulating actually...you know, inspiring!

G. Inspiring? Well, yes, I suppose it was...a bit. But I ask you, is that why we go to church, to be inspired?

H. Yes, partly.

G. But it was all so...so...

H. Different?

G. Yes, different. I don't like change, especially not in church!

H. We've got to move with the times...

G. Yes, but not if it includes hymns that we don't know, and all that drama business, and what about all that touching and moving about?

H. You mean the Sharing of the Peace?

G. Is that what they call it? More like a cattle market. I don't go to church to be touched by my neighbours. I don't go to church to be touched by *anything*!

H. Give them a chance. They've only made one or two changes and they were very sensitive in introducing them. I can't remember when I last enjoyed worship so much, and I felt so close to God during that dance. Can't wait 'till next week!

G. I'm not sure I'll be there next week. If they think these new ideas are going to help the church grow, they must be _mad_!

(They freeze)

(A and B come to life again and continue to talk as they stroll across the stage)

A. So, how did it go with Louise? Did she give you an ear-bashing?

B. No, she was quite calm really. A bit nervous, you know, on edge. But we managed to sort things out...

A. Did you? That's amazing!

B. Yeah! It felt really strange at first, I mean, I didn't really know how she would react, but we couldn't have continued the way we were for much longer. One of us had to hold out a hand of friendship, and I thought, "why not me?"

A. Good for you! I saw Louise at the bus stop this morning. She looked so relaxed! Looks like you've made a difference!

(They freeze)

(C and D come to life and stroll to another position as they talk)

C. How's Mission Impossible going then?
D. Sorry? *(C makes sign for money)* Oh, the fund raising...
C. Are we into double figures yet?
D. Bit better than that, didn't you hear about the Commitment Day we had last week? Nearly everyone in the congregation turned out, and some others as well, and they have pledged so generously! Some have covenanted their gifts and some have even promised a chunk of their income!
C. Really? Well, I did hear the sermon last week - it nearly burnt a hole in *my* pocket!
D. Yes, the Day of Prayer was very special too. All these things are really making a difference!

(They freeze)

(E and F come to life and walk to a vacant position as they talk)

E. I still can't understand why you want to go all that way!
F. Well, I just feel that God is calling me there...it's like a yearning that won't go away... it's something I've got to do.
E. But why?
F. I suppose it's because I realise how much I've been given by God and now I want to show how grateful I am...give something back.
E. But you could do that *here*!
F. True, but the travel and adventure are very attractive too. They seem to reflect where I am in my faith. I'm looking for challenge, not comfort!
E. Well, it's not for me, I'm afraid.
F. That's O.K. There are lots of exciting ways you can express your faith and serve God here at home, and they all make a difference.

(They freeze)

(G and H come to life...)

G. Arrrh, it's lovely at St Lukewarm's. We have all the old hymns, and a proper sermon, not too long, and nobody ever troubles you or makes demands. Everybody is so thoughtful that they haven't spoken to me once yet!
H. I'm glad you're happy. I began to worry about you when I didn't see you at church.
G. How are things up there?
H. Fine! The Junior Church is growing, and the youth group led worship again last Sunday. They even got me to dig out my clarinet to join the new worship band! It's wonderful! And yesterday, the minister invited all the young people

to sit next to an older person and for everyone to learn as much as they could about each other in five minutes! We laughed and cried, and discovered so much! Anyway, I can't stop, we're loading a lorry with aid for Bosnian refugees this afternoon.

G. I still can't see what all this has to do with Christianity...

H. Well, that's just it. We didn't hear a sermon about being the body of Christ, we actually experienced what it means! We're not just preaching the message, we're trying to put into practice! I'm sure that's why so many are coming back to church lately. You have to get there early to get a seat most Sundays! Honestly, these things are really making a difference!

(They freeze)

(Each character springs to life and walks towards the audience shouting their lines...)

A. Mad people!
B. Mad churches!
C. Mad dreams!
D. Mad visions!
E. Mad ideas!
F. Mad standards!
G. Mad behaviour!
H. Mad lifestyles!

A. *Making A Difference* people!
B. *Making A Difference* churches!
C. *Making A Difference* dreams and visions!
D. *Making A Difference* ideas and standards!

E. Behaviour that *Makes A Difference*!
F. Lifestyles that *Make A Difference*!
G. In quiet, small, gentle ways!
H. In loud, large earth-shattering ways!

A. In the beginning...
B. God *Made A Difference*!
C. Through Abraham and Moses...
D. God *Made A Difference*!
E. With the words of the prophets...
F. God *Made A Difference*!
G. God so loved the world that...
H. God *Made A Difference*!

A. When the day of Pentecost came...
All: God *Made A Difference*!

B. No guarantees...
C. No certainty of success...
D. No worldly security...

E.   No status symbols...
F.   But all the adventure...
G.   All the excitement...
H.   All the challenge of being God's people in the world!

A.   Abraham?
All: *MAD!*
B.   Moses?
All: *MAD!*
C.   The prophets?
All: *MAD!*
D.   John the Baptist?
All: *MAD!*
E.   Jesus?

(Sudden silence. Characters all look at each other, puzzled)

E.   Yeah, they accused even Jesus of being mad...
F.   And the disciples at Pentecost...
G.   And Paul...
H.   And as for the church today, well...

(All characters look out at the audience, scanning the faces, searching...)

(They freeze)

Malcolm Hanson and Martin John Nicholls

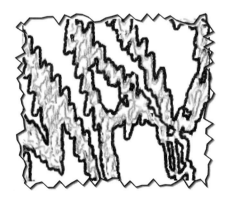

The Orchestra of Christ

A Paraphrase of 1 Corinthians 12. 12-26, many young people identify with the imagery used here.
It can be read in chorus, with different voices accentuating certain words or lines.

Christ is like an orchestra,
which has many musicians;
it is still one orchestra even though it is made up
of different instruments.
In the same way, all of us,
whether black or white,
male or female,
young or old,
wealthy or poor,
sharp or flat,
have been invited to play in concert.

The orchestra is not made up of only one instrument,
but of many instruments:
If the drum was to say,
"because I am not a violin, I don't belong to the orchestra"
that would not keep it from playing its part in the music;
and if the guitar was to say,
"because I am not a clarinet, I don't belong to the orchestra"
that would not keep it from playing its part in the music.

If the whole orchestra was made up of bagpipes
how could it play rock and roll;
and if the whole orchestra was made up of tambourines
how could it play Beethoven's Ninth?

So, the conductor has put every instrument and musician
just where he wants them.
There would not be an orchestra if it were all one harmonica.
As it is, there are many instruments, but one orchestra.

So, the trombone cannot say to the triangle,
"I don't need you!"
Nor can the bassoon say to the banjo,
"I don't need you!"
On the contrary, we cannot do without
the parts of the orchestra that seem weaker,
and those instruments which we think aren't worth very much
(like the grade 2 recorders,)
are the ones which we treat with greater care.

God himself has put the orchestra together so that
greater honour is given to those instruments that need it,
like the washboard or Peruvian nose flute.
And so there is no discord in the orchestra
but all the musicians play sensitively,
listening to each other.

If one instrument is out of tune,
the whole orchestra suffers.
If one instrument plays a beautiful solo,
the whole orchestra shares in the ovation.

All of you are Christ's orchestra
and each of you has a part to play

...in harmony.

Composer God

Composer God,
Orchestrator of Creation,
you have drawn us together,
unveiled our skills,
and given us the instruments.
Now you invite us to play
your melody of love.

You have set the time and key;
you have written the arrangement and lyrics.
The words and music are yours alone.

The universe moves to your divine rhythm;
Atoms dance to your counterpoint;
Seasons and tides,
days and nights ebb and flow
to your tempo.

In the cries from a cradle,
the crash of a cloud-burst,
the crackle of a camp-fire
and the crunch of crisp snow;
we hear the symphony of life.

You stand before us now,
baton raised in readiness
for the overture of praise.
We wait,
eager, excited,
to perform your masterpiece,
"The Kingdom."

This is a dream come true;
a lifelong ambition:
to play our part under your
personal direction!

We are ready, Maestro,
to watch your every move;
to give of our best;
to do justice to your work,
and to relish the harmony.

Move us with the music of your mercy.

The field of dreams...

A short liturgy based upon the tiny parables of discovery Jesus gives us in Matthew's Gospel.
Focal points of ears of wheat, seeds and soil can be placed in a central position or passed
round during the prayers.

We adore you, Sower God
for planting your Word in our hearts and minds.
We worship you, Farmer God
for making room for the wheat and the weeds.
We love you, Astonishing God
for continuing to surprise and delight us.

God of the field and the fire place,
tools and treasures,
thank you for unearthing your Kingdom for us.

Matthew 13. Verses 24-30.

In the birth-cry a new day
and the safe embrace of night fall;
> *In the caring conversation of friends*
> *and the tender caress of a loved one;*
In the soaring and in the soil
your world shouts aloud:
> *"God's Kingdom is come!"*
Forgive our arrogance and prejudice;
our familiarity which breeds contempt.
> *Make us good stewards of all your fruitful gifts;*
> *Make us worthy of the trust you place in us;*
Uncover the treasure within us
> *So that others may celebrate life*
> *and worship you.*
We are yours, rich and ready for the harvest:
> *By your Spirit transform us*
> *from a field of failure and frustration*
> *into a field of dreams.*

Matthew 13. Verses 31 and 32.

There is a longing and a loneliness
> *Until we are reconciled to you;*
There is a yearning and a hunger
> *Until your will is done;*
There is a passion and a burning
> *Until your justice and peace prevail;*
There is nothing
> *Until there is love.*

Matthew 13. Verse 44.

God of such love and longing,
Why do you sow your seeds of justice
if not to allow them to grow to their full potential?
    Why do you scatter your visions
    if not to give us a purpose?
Why do you give us such dreams
if not to show us how to make them real?
    Why do you plant kernels of possibility
    if not to fill the world with peace?
Why do you show us hidden treasures
if not to give us the honour of claiming the field for you?
    Yours is the Kingdom, sovereign Lord!
    Yours is the power, mighty God!
    Yours is the glory, eternal Love!
    Amen! Amen! AMEN!

Take Time!

People of all ages have difficulty in using time wisely - even finding the time to pray! This worship experience explores some of those problems. A collection of clocks and watches (all stopped) make a powerful focal point, surrounded by a collection of fallen leaves - symbols of the passing seasons.

The sun rises and the sun goes down
Then hurries to the place where it rises again.
The wind blows to the south, and then to the north,
Round and round it blows, only to return.
The streams all run to the sea, but the sea is not full,
The seas rise as mists and then to clouds only to rain into streams.
What has been is what will be,
And what has been done is what will be done.
Is there one thing which is truly new?
There is nothing new under the sun!

Based upon Ecclesiastes 1. 4-10

A song

How Time Flies! We all remove our watches, place them in a central place then close our eyes. We are then asked to try and gauge (or guess) the passing of one minute, which one person will monitor carefully using their watch.

When we think a minute has passed, we should put up our hand and open our eyes. Note should be taken of when the hands are raised in relation to the minute. Everyone's idea of time will be different! Feel free to share your feelings about the passing of time and how hard it is to use time wisely. Depending on circumstances and experiences, time can appear to drag or fly, and yet, it remains virtually constant. A minute, is a minute, is a minute!

Think of as many phrases as possible, which are used everyday, concerning time (make time, spend time, save time...)
It is not how much time we have, but what we do with that time that matters.

Words of Affirmation:

For every thing there is a right time
And a time for every thing under heaven:
A time to be born,
And a time to die;
A time to plant,
And a time to harvest;
A time to build,
And a time to demolish
A time to cry,
And a time to laugh!
A time to grieve,
And a time to dance!

A time to scatter,
 And a time to gather;
A time to embrace,
 And a time to give space;
A time to search,
 And a time to lose;
A time to keep,
 And a time to let go;
A time to be quiet,
 AND A TIME TO SHOUT!

Based on Ecclesiastes 3. 1-7

Imagine that the next 5 minutes were your last. What would you do with them? What would be your priorities? Actually, the next 5 minutes are totally unique, they have never been seen before and, once they have passed, they will never be seen again! They are very precious...

God's Word: Luke 12. 22-31.

God of all time and this time,
 Of every place and this place,
Of all life and our lives;
 You are the God of eternity
Yet you alone show me perfect love;
 A love which knows when to give and when to receive;
A love which knows when to hold and when to let go;
 A love which know no limit and counts no cost;
A love which allows itself to die for the sake of others.
 We have seen that love in a human life.
 His name is Jesus.

Everyone comes forward and chooses a leaf from the centre, then returns to their place and holds the leaf out in front of them.

By your Holy Spirit, give us the wisdom to know
the right times and the right places.
 By your grace, give us the courage to let go
 of all that hinders, worries or distracts us.
That this might be your time
 That this might be your time
That this might be your place
 That this might be your place
That this might be your life
 That this might be your life
 Let it be so -
 For it is time!

In the silence, each person lets go of their leaf, allowing it to fall to the ground, as a symbol of releasing their worries and distractions as they focus upon God's Kingdom.

All depart in silence

Airs and Graces
Some lively "Thank You" songs for meal times at camps or youth events

---

Rock Around The Cook
Can be sung to the tune of "Rock Around The Clock"

God, you're great!
God, you're good!
And we thank you for our food,
we're gonna thank you morning, noon and night,
we're gonna thank you 'cause you're dynamite!
Amen! *(clap, clap)*
Amen! *(clap, clap)*
Amen! *(clap, clap, clap, clap, clap, clap)*

Adam's Family
Can be sung to the tune of The Adams family

(Da, da, da, da, click click)

O Lord, we're really grateful
for every cup and plateful;
forgive us when we're wasteful
'cause we're your family.

You guide us and lead us;
you strengthen us and feed us
to live and love like Jesus
'cause we're your family.

(da, da, da, da, Thank God!...)

We Love Breakfast!

Can be sung to the tune of "The Flintstones"

Cornflakes, or Rice Crispies
or some muesli or some Weetabix;
Frosties, tea or coffee,
we have such a choice to pick and mix!
Thank you
for the snap, crackle, and pop!
Toast with
jam or marmalade on top!
Breakfast, we love breakfast,
it's a yummy, yummy, yum time,
it's fill your tum, time,
so we say thank you, Lord!

Hey, Lord!

Can be sung to the tune of "Hey Jude"

Hey, Lord!
we come to praise
and adore you for all you're giving.
You feed us in body mind and soul,
calling us all to life worth living.
O, Lord,
we come in faith,
in the name of Jesus our Saviour.
We pray for
all those in need of our care;
help us to share you food and flavour.
Nar, nar, nar, na na na na, na na na na,
praise God!....

Super Food

Can be sung to the tune of "Superman"

Thank you, God,
for being so good!
Thank you, God,
for brilliant food!
And we praise you
and adore you
in your Holy name,
Amen!

Super food
and wonderful friends!
Super love
that never ends!
Super Father!
Super Spirit!
Super Jesus Christ
is Lord!

O Salad Mio!

Can be sung to the tune "O Sole Mio"

Just one tomato, give it to me,
and some cucumber and celery.
A salad is so healthy
and baked potatoes are good for me.
Give me some coleslaw,
radish as well,
onions are tasty, but make me smell!
Before you walk away,
thank God for salad
(big finish)
and lettuce pray!

An Amazing Grace
(For after a meal)
Can be sing to the tune "Amazing Grace"

An amazing grace
that's what this is,
for an amazing meal!
I once was empty,
now I'm full.
God knows how full I feel!

I want to thank you,
living Lord,
you call, you guide, you feed.
Help me to share
your love and care
with those who are in need!

Summer Bites
Can be sung to the tune "Summer Nights"

(Dum da dum, da dum, da dum dum dum dum.
Da dum da dum da dum dum dum dum)
Some are fond of jelly and cream;
Some just fill their belly and dream;
Some prefer a fruity milk shake;
Some pig out on chocolate cake.
Yummy sweets are easy to eat, but, *(uh,)*
we have more than we need!
(A wella, wella, wella, uh!)
Thank you, Lord, thank you, Lord,
for the food we have got!
Help us Lord, help us Lord,
share with those who have not!